THE
2012
GRIFFIN
POETRY
PRIZE
ANTHOLOGY

PAST WINNERS OF
THE GRIFFIN POETRY PRIZE

2001
Anne Carson
Heather McHugh and
Nikolai Popov

2002
Christian Bök
Alice Notley

2003
Margaret Avison
Paul Muldoon

2004
August Kleinzahler
Anne Simpson

2005
Roo Borson
Charles Simic

2006
Kamau Brathwaite
Sylvia Legris

2007
Don McKay
Charles Wright

2008
John Ashbery
Robin Blaser

2009
A. F. Moritz
C. D. Wright

2010
Eiléan Ní Chuilleanáin
Karen Solie

2011
Dionne Brand
Gjertrud Schnackenberg

The 2012 Griffin Poetry Prize Anthology

A SELECTION OF THE SHORTLIST

Edited by DAVID O'MEARA

Copyright © 2012 House of Anansi Press Inc.
Poems copyright © individual poets
Preface copyright © David O'Meara

All rights reserved. No part of this publication may be reproduced or transmitted in any form or by any means, electronic or mechanical, including photocopying, recording, or any information storage and retrieval system, without permission in writing from the publisher.

This edition published in 2012 by
House of Anansi Press Inc.
110 Spadina Avenue, Suite 801
Toronto, ON, M5V 2K4
Tel. 416-363-4343
Fax 416-363-1017
www.houseofanansi.com

Distributed in Canada by	Distributed in the United States by
HarperCollins Canada Ltd.	Publishers Group West
1995 Markham Road	1700 Fourth Street
Scarborough, ON, M1B 5M8	Berkeley, CA 94710
Toll free tel. 1-800-387-0117	Toll free tel. 1-800-788-3123

House of Anansi Press is committed to protecting our natural environment. As part of our efforts, the interior of this book is printed on paper made from second-growth forests and is acid free.

16 15 14 13 12   1 2 3 4 5

Library and Archives Canada Cataloguing in Publication

Cataloguing data available from Library and Archives Canada

Library of Congress Control Number: 2011945360

Cover design: Brian Morgan
Cover image: Mimmo Jodice, *Apollo di Baia*, 1993. Silver print on baryta paper, edition of eight. 50 x 60 cm. Courtesy Galerie Karsten Greve
Typesetting: Alysia Shewchuk

We acknowledge for their financial support of our publishing program the Canada Council for the Arts, the Ontario Arts Council, and the Government of Canada through the Canada Book Fund.

Printed and bound in Canada

"Poetry is the past that breaks out in our hearts."
—Rainer Maria Rilke

CONTENTS

Preface, by David O'Meara / xi

INTERNATIONAL FINALISTS

DAVID HARSENT, *Night*
   A View of the House from the Back of the Garden / 5
   Blood Alley / 6
   Scene One: A Beach / 7
   Spatchcock / 11
   Blue / 13
   Contre-jour / 14

YUSEF KOMUNYAKAA, *The Chameleon Couch*
   The Story of a Coat / 21
   When Eyes Are On Me / 23
   Poppies / 25
   Three Figures at the Base of a Crucifixion / 27
   Last of the Monkey Gods / 28
   A Visit to Inner Sanctum / 29

SEAN O'BRIEN, *November*
  Sunk Island / 33
  Josie / 34
  The Citizens / 35
  White Enamel Jug / 36
  The Lost Book / 37
  Europeans / 41
  Counting the Rain / 42
  Closed / 43

JOANNA TRZECIAK, *translator*
TADEUSZ RÓŻEWICZ, **Sobbing Superpower: Selected Poems of Tadeusz Różewicz**
  Unde malum? / 47
  Homework Assignment on the Subject of Angels / 49
  Love Toward the Ashes / 51
  Pig Roast / 54
  Sobbing Superpower / 57
  Chiaroscuro / 61

CANADIAN FINALISTS

KEN BABSTOCK, *Methodist Hatchet*
The Decor / 67
Autumn News from the Donkey Sanctuary / 71
Which Helmet? / 73
Hoping Your Machine Can Handle the Big Image / 74
Avalon, Helicopter / 77

PHIL HALL, *Killdeer*
A Thin Plea / 81

JAN ZWICKY, *Forge*
Practicing Bach / 91
When You Look Up / 97
Schumann: Fantasie, Op. 17 / 98
Gemini / 100

About the Poets / 103
About the Judges / 107
Acknowledgements / 109

PREFACE

Fiona Sampson, Heather McHugh and I received 481 books, in the original English or in translation, to concentrate our minds through the winter months of 2011–2012. Taken from the boxes, the books were stacked and restacked. To find the best ones involved persistence but the search was a tremendously invigorating and rewarding experience. This unique collection of books was a record of one year in the life of our planet, concentrated through the vigilant, generous minds of a cross-section of our poets. Their poems contained the memories of our past and what we imagine our futures will be, exploring the wreckage of history, studying our personal hopes and political failures, exposing the vigorous lives of our minds. But the question lingered with each cracked cover: which books did it best and why?

The reasons why a book of poetry is successful are as varied as the reasons why it doesn't succeed. The demands on skill and balance are enormous. If the poet were a juggler you might hope he or she would not only keep six bowling pins in the air, but a chainsaw and a feather as well, perhaps while riding a unicycle. If really good, the juggler might wow us with a few jokes, or by lighting a cigar. With poetry, you are looking for the finest combination of effects, structurally and stylistically, beyond mere accomplishment. As a reader you want to experience a culmination of skill: to hear that language has been considered and pressured, that familiar things are described in an unfamiliar way, that an image has seemingly dropped out of the clear blue sky and hit you so hard you see flashing lights. You want leaps of imagination and logic. You want poems to be tough, beautiful, unfair, irreverent, jarringly weird and suddenly clear. You don't want a poem to tell you how to feel; you want it to describe an experience so vividly that you also live it. In all of this, the poet must be continually versatile. "Strength lies in improvisation," as Walter Benjamin wrote. "The blows that count are all landed with the left." The choice between bombast and restraint presents itself at every word, and as the game changes with new images or shifts in tone, you are also asking the poet to exercise tact. So any attempt at spectacle can be abandoned for quieter, graceful notes if the effect will be more memorable, as if our juggler, at the height of performance, dropped everything to perform a tea ceremony.

Each of the shortlisted books is exemplary, and they are excellent for different reasons. If Joanna Trzeciak's translations of Tadeusz Różewicz's poems faithfully reproduce the blunt diction of his lines, then the incantatory sensuousness of Yusef Komunyakaa's verse communicates skepticism in an equally effective way. Just as Jan Zwicky's dynamic is to contain simple vocabulary inside an obsessive, cumulative set of yearnings, Ken Babstock's volcanic play of image and association suggests the volatility of perception. We experience Sean O'Brien's combination of atmosphere and metric eloquence quite differently than David Harsent's post-crisis psychological fixations (a kind of *Havisham noir*), or Phil Hall's courageous balance of intellect and feeling. In our winter of reading, we enjoyed many fine poems. We judged these seven books the best and it's a pleasure to bring these poets together in this anthology, which is like a dinner party of exceptional, interesting guests. Their voices tell us stories, rattle our complacency, remind us of our compassion, dazzle us with language, and never bore us. They invite and engage us in conversation, maybe the finest you'll have this year.

David O'Meara, March 2012

INTERNATIONAL
FINALISTS

DAVID HARSENT

Night

David Harsent conducts an examination of the human psyche that is unique in both the unflinchingness of its gaze, and the fabular metaphors it uses to explore dream, terror and hidden impulse. Truly significant poets write like no one else, and Harsent is both *sui generis* and unsurpassed. In *Night* an extraordinary imaginary is evoked, explored and even wrought by technique that shows its hand only gradually, as the patterning of rhythmic urges and sound-chimes reveals how extraordinarily through-composed the book is. This is at the same time poetry of supreme urgency, haunted by existential and contemporary necessities in which the homeless man in the underpass, the wild "Goddess" of back gardens, are trickster archetypes — and are our neighbours, too. A collection of tremendous rhythmic and formal variety, one which ranges from a set of colourist "Abstracts" to a ballad, is dominated, but never overshadowed, by its last quarter. Extraordinarily sustained, with more than four hundred lines composed in septets lightly patterned with slant, blanket stitch and internal rhymes, "Elsewhere" is quite simply a canonical poem. It is also a quest narrative that, like all Harsent's work, seems to pass right through its own genre, and return us to its origins in psychodrama and rite.

A View of the House from the Back of the Garden

In darkness. In rain. Yourself at the very point
where what's yours bleeds off through the palings
to *terra incognita*, and the night's blood-hunt
starts up in the brush: the notion of something smiling
as it slinks in now for the rush and sudden shunt.

A woman is laying a table; the cloth
billows as it settles; a wine-glass catches the light.
A basket for bread, spoons and bowls for broth
as you know, just as you know how slight
a hold you have on this: a lit window, the faint
odour of iodine in the rainfall's push and pull.

Now she looks out, but you're invisible
as you planned, though maybe it's a failing
to stand at one remove, to watch, to want
everything stalled and held on an indrawn breath.

The house, the woman, the window, the lamplight falling
short of everything except bare earth —
can you see how it seems, can you tell
why you happen to be just here, where the garden path
runs off to black, still watching
as she turns away, sharply, as if in fright,
while the downpour thickens and her shadow on the wall,
trembling, is given over to the night?

Surely it's that moment from the myth
in which you look back and everything goes to hell.

Blood Alley

Your childhood token, a sickle of red in the glass, albino eye,
eye of the night-lamped hare; a perfect lob would break the circle…

Now hold it close to the light and every fibril
seems to shred, as heart-blood hangs in water, that same dark dye —

shade of the dress she wore when you had your first full taste
of the pulp of her lip and the spittle off her tongue, the cost

to you being more than you had to give, which is why
the circle must break again and the dream unpick and the child
    be lost.

Scene One: A Beach

I

And this is where I've got to, pitched up on some shoreline
like any piece of wreckage, like something
once adrift, now simply lost, no given purpose,
no way of knowing where from, where to, no sense of direction,
just this notion of distance covered, this notion of release,
at what might be nightfall, might be daybreak, but no sign
to tell me which, no help at hand, only the subtle traction
of a rising tide nudging me up and on as if the thing
to do is get clear, get going, as if somewhere yet unseen
but only a short way off might prove to be the place
I'd always had in mind, as if a voice still waiting
to be heard might give me a start, perhaps a word
to work with, and I might somehow conjure a face
from a cloud and that sudden vision tell me everything.

II

I can hear the breakers and a rush of wings,
that's all. I can get to my feet. I can take the first
full step. I can open my eyes. I can see how light is cast
under the fold of the wave and how it hangs
forward of the water when it falls. As for the rest,
there's only the blur and hum that always lies
at the near side of what comes next, or what is past.

III

Begin in silence, the sea drawn back
to a distant smudge beneath a fading moon.
Shingle first, then turf and soon the seamless black
of a road that rolls to the edge, then on to stolen ground.
Everything I once recognised as mine
is strange to me now, and that stupendous lack

is what gives me my pace, what helps me on
towards the unheard, the invisible, the rare,
subtle as tears in rainfall, as breath on the wind...
The road delivers me. The residue of prayer
lies on my lip like salt. The place is dust
in a bowl of barren hills. A voice declares
*Your starting point is grief; you must
get used to this.* To being out of mind; to being moonblind.

IV
Go from here, go from the shoreline again,
the sun just up, frost on the open ground, a blue
haze in the distance that must be the city's spew.
I'm at odds with myself; I shift, somehow, in my skin;
my bones are wrong; my eye-line's out of true...
What next? I'll follow the long thin line
of my shadow until I find somewhere to get to.

V
Now this house on the outskirts: its bald, blind look,
and a room in the house where someone sits
barely breathing, hands folded, eyes wide, and waits
for the sound of a voice, perhaps, or the sound of a lock
turning, someone whose view of the window gives back
only night-day-night; but here's my face at the glass
to observe the white walls, the bare floor, the seated figure,
to return that steady stare, to deliver like for like,
as if a question might be put, as if something might pass
between us that would give me the clue to the room,
to the left-over traces of night, shadows that gather
in corners, a silence that could split along its seam...
Time out of time; one reflection laid on the other.
I turn away as if I were turning from home.

VI

Rain off the sea, a sudden rush that smothers
the long line of the beach and turns it dark…
Rumble of stones in the undertow, dreck
scummed up at the tideline, oil and feathers,
the sky near-touchable, a rising wind at my back.
One horizon sliding towards me, and another
lost in blue however far I walk.

VII

Into the city grid, streets slammed down thus
by the Planner's iron hand which means you can go
only this way or that, and two by two
as intended, just like myself and whoever it is
walking beside me, silent, looking down
so as not to miss a step. There are houses with doors
but no windows, or sometimes it's windows
and no doors. Wherever they go they're in the zone
and seem to know it by the worried smiles, the eyes
closing for a moment as they pass. There are no trees
in the city square, or cafés, or fountains. Here they lean
on each other's arms, or hover in mid-stride
as, for a moment, do I, does he, until I step aside
knowing whoever he is he's better left alone.

VIII

Spindrift, skim of the sea torn off to fall just short
of where I'm knees-to-chin, arms wrapped about me, caught
in the lee of a breakwater, wondering how to get
the best out of this, how to tell the way back from the way
forward, if only by day, in good weather, if only by starlight.
The gulls are screaming, not weeping as people like to say.
There's nothing to hope for in this, and nothing to regret.

IX
A valley seen from a hillside, beyond which
a plain rolling out a chequerboard of rocks
and scrub beyond which a wood that quickly thins
to swamp beyond which a glint from tower blocks
beyond which a landscape showing no more than stitch
and patch from this distance through which runs
the only road, the road I've followed, it seems,
to the end and then beyond. In the valley, a river
of souls; on the plain, a sun-bleached cadaver;
in the wood, a gallows-branch; in the swamp a hand
reaching out; in the tower block a murder
that always goes unseen... and no surprise to find
a figure in that landscape, hammered by suns,
constantly going forward, constantly losing ground.

X
The ocean churns its junk of bones, its tar
and toxins, whatever might break
the surface of the menstruum, bald and white, whatever
beaches here, mongrel or throwback,
something just skin and finger, something just beak
and gill. All that rouses me now is fret and fever
and all that concerns me how deep, how dark, how far.

Spatchcock

As I entered, she had her pinking shears to the backbone,
having dropped the gizzard into the kitchen bin,
and barely looked over her shoulder to see who it was

when I gave the door a little back-heel
then ferreted round in the fridge for an ice-cold Coors
before slipping up from behind to cop a feel.

Another hot day in September, and that the cause
of her half-baked look, brought on
by lying bare-assed in the garden all afternoon,

a flush coming off her, the veins so close to the skin
I could trace the flow like sap, could tongue-up the ooze
of sweat at the nape of her neck: and this the real

taste of her, like nothing before, like nothing I ever knew.
You have to go hard at it, either side of the spine,
all the time bearing down against the sinew,

then lift the long bone entire and get both hands
into the cut, knuckle to knuckle, and draw
the carcass apart, and press, till you hear the breastbone crack.

Looked at like that it's roadkill, flat on its back,
sprung ribcage, legs akimbo, red side up, and sends
a message (you might guess) about life lived in the raw.

So then it's a matter of taste: herb-butter under the slack
of the breast, perhaps, or a tart marinade,
to flatter and blend, spread thinly and rubbed well in.

She favoured the latter — that and a saltire of thin
skewers driven aslant from thigh to neck,
which might, indeed, have said something about her mood.

That done, she stripped off, gathering the oils and the balm
she'd need for however long the thing would take,
and went back to her place in the sun. It did no harm,

I suppose, to watch from an upstairs window: a hawk's-
eye-view as she lay there timing the turn
(face-up till you tingle, then flip) to brown but not to burn.

The marks of the griddle, the saltire, the subtle flux...
We ate it with lima beans and picked the bones,
after which we took to bed a bottle of bright Sancerre

and I held her down as I'd held her down before,
working her hot-spots with a certain caution and care
as she told me not here... or here... but there... and *there*.

I left her flat on her back and shedding a glow,
or so I like to think, as I slipped downstairs
and lifted, from a peg-board beside the hob,

her mother's (or grandmother's) longhand note on how
to spatchcock a chicken, or guinea, or quail, or squab,
or sparrow, even, with emphasis on that 'crack';

and lifted, as well, before I lifted the latch,
myrtle, borage, dill, marjoram, tarragon, sumac,
all named and tagged in a customized cardboard box.

Blue

It sings they say, and so it does: something like the note
that fractures glass or gets so far below
the range of human hearing that it shakes your heart;

and the glass it breaks is blue, and that's a blue note for sure
from the guy on the alto sax in the basement dive,
which is where they're bound to meet up in the classic *noir*,

the private eye, the girl with a shadowy past, the old-style cop,
and it's nigh-on certain she'll have to take a bullet
or we'll see her in prison blue as they lead her to the drop.

The fragments of glass were part of it too, that's plain,
though no one noticed, just as they failed to spot
how the crucifix in her bedroom made sense of the subtle stain

on her cocktail dress. And in this, the director's cut,
the dive is deeper, the saxophone sadder, the cop
bent as a dog's hind leg, the girl a scheming slut,

and the gumshoe comes in late with the one and only clue
that would finally set things straight, though its true
meaning is hidden from him, and lost on you.

Contre-jour

Dark-blue of dawn, deserted streets,
a light fall of soot in the rain, a man out alone, the faint

asdic of his footfalls off the pavement, the city
stirring round him, rumble of engines underground

or what might be a furnace starting up...A dawn
like any other, a nowhere city, the man myself.

~

I could tell I was cold, I could tell I was lost, I could feel
the grit from a sleepless night under my eyelids

and that slow, sour churn in the gut
of cheapjack wine. Morning shadows rolled

low along gutters and sills, like ground-mist shrouding
the gods of the black back-alleys, gods of the threshold.

~

I remembered a half-remembered dream of falling,
the sky on fire, cloud-wrack a bled bruise, wingbeats

drumming the wind. Blind and breathless. Numb
to my fingertips. I spread my arms and howled and trod plain air.

My descent was a kind of dance. The shadow shifted.
When I came to the cross-street I knew which way to go.

~

The underpass stank of sleepers. Trucks overhead
had opened a web of fault-lines that carried a dark dew:

enough to root pale, pin-head flowers. A man got up
from his mess of bedding, then, and kept pace with me,

unspeaking, his eyes on the light ahead, but he reached
out and picked me a flower: it brightened as the stem snapped.

~

He walked me as far as the river and left me there.
The cloud broke. Sunlight surged on the water and ran to black

by factory footings. A bell began. I seemed to see him again
clean-cutting the surface, feet first from the bridge,

past hulls and anchor chains… and days of drifting
before he snagged, wide-eyed, on the river's sunken iron.

~

By wharves and warehouses; gulls on the garbage scow;
the graffiti was all about love and remedies for love.

Stone steps took me into the backstreets; there came a cry
of pleasure or pain from an open window, and something in that

I seemed to recognise: not the voice, not the place,
but the way she broke off as if it might come to laughter.

~

The city square at midday, raked by light from a cloud.
A skinny dog went through, bone cranking bone.

A café on one side; on the other, a church…
And suppose I might have been content with that,

a splash of neon, the rose window, unanswered silence…
Suppose I might have found a way to sit and wait.

~

The memory's long since lost, but still there's a sense
of someone at my shoulder, of someone beyond the door,

of a voice somehow trapped in the room, although the words
are shuffled and split; or there's something barely held,

a photograph gone grey, as if dusk had blotted everything
except for a shape out of shadow turning towards the night.

~

The city as stone and steel, as silt and litter. Those moments
when the roar from the grid holds off, a dynamo winding down,

and the sorrowing call to each other through the birdsong.
I got to the edge and turned. The backdrop sky was white;

for just that moment, everything stood in negative:
the whole place mapped onto itself; the city as guesswork…

~

Petrol haze on the bypass. Wayside shrines
of the accident black-spots, votives catching the wind.

I'd been on the road a while before I felt
a sense of loss, or was it need of forgiveness? Even now

there are times when I wonder if that was the least of it:
the bridge, her cry, a flower drawn from darkness.

YUSEF KOMUNYAKAA

The Chameleon Couch

Alter egos, second selves figure largely in Komunyakaa's new poetry collection, *The Chameleon Couch*. In "The Hedonist," successive masks are donned and discarded to feed the speaker's voracious appetite for experience, as throughout the book, personae are adopted — The Window Dresser, Adonis, Orpheus, the "Ten or Eleven Disguises," a Mr. Decoy — to bear witness to the continual bartering of good and evil that comprise the fallen mythic world of the book's vision. Both speaking from direct experience and with the collective scrutiny of our shared civilization, where ages and cultures overlap, in the "scuffle / between gods and human shadows," the poems roam contemporary streets to the edges of crumbling empires, where the restless ghosts of history still linger on the corner. Beneath these masks, and central to the success of these poems, is Komunyakaa's singular voice: curious, doubtful, stubborn, damning and self-accusing, asserting itself against the never-tiring devastation wrought by history, its testimony "good as making a wager against the eternal hush. "

The Story of a Coat

We talked about Baroness Pannonica
driving her Silver Pigeon to the Five Spot
to chauffeur Monk home. I was happy
not to talk football, the inventory of skulls
in a cave in Somalia, the democratic vistas
of the Cedar Tavern, or about Spinoza.
We were saying how the legs go first,
& then from the eyes mystery is stolen.
I said how much I miss Bill Matthews,
that sometimes at the Village Vanguard,
Fez, or Smalls, especially when some cat
steals a riff out of Prez's left back pocket,
I hear his Cincinnati laugh. Then our gaze
snagged on a green dress shifting the light.
If you'd asked me, I couldn't have said why
I knew jasmine from the silence of Egypt,
or how water lives only to remember fire.
As we walked out of the sanctuary of garlic,
chive, onion, mushroom, & peppery dough,
we agreed Rahsaan could see rhythm
when he blew wounded cries of night hawks
at daybreak. The heat of the pizza parlor
followed us to the corner, & two steps later
I remembered the scent of loneliness
in my coat left draped over the chair.
I had fallen in love with its cut,
how it made me walk straighter.
When I passed the young James Dean
coming out the door with my blue-gray coat
balled up in his arms, I didn't stop him.
I don't know why. I just stood there
at the table. But, David, years after

I circled the globe, I'm still ashamed
of memories that make me American
as music made of harmony & malice.

When Eyes Are On Me

I am a scrappy old lion
who's wandered into a Christian square
quavering with centuries of forged bells.
The cobblestones make my feet ache.

I walk big-shouldered, my head raised
proudly. I smell the blood of a king.
The citizens can see only a minotaur in a maze.
I know more than a lion should know.

My roar goes back to the Serengeti,
to when a savanna was craggy ice,
but now it frightens only pigeons from a city stoop.
They believe they know my brain's contours & grammar.

Don't ask me how I know the signs engraved
on a sundial, the secret icons behind a gaze.
I wish their crimes hadn't followed me here.
I can hear their applause in the dusty citadel.

I know what it took to master the serpent
& wheel, the crossbow & spinal tap.
Once I was a leopard beside a stone gate.
I am a riddle to be unraveled. I am not

& I am. When their eyes are on me
I become whatever is judged badly.
I circle the park. Hunger shapes
my keen sense of smell, a lifetime ahead.

They will follow my pawprints
till they're lost in snow at dusk.
If I walk in circles, I hide from my shadow.
They plot stars to know where to find me.

I am a prodigal bird perched on the peak
of a guardhouse. I have a message
for fate. The sunlight has shown me
the guns, & their beautiful sons are deadly.

Poppies

These frantic blooms can hold their own
when it comes to metaphor & God.
Take any name or shade of irony, any flowery
indifference or stolen gratitude, & our eyes,
good or bad, still run up to this hue.
Take this woman sitting beside me,

a descendant of Hungarian Gypsies
born to teach horses to dance & eat sugar
from her hand, does she know beauty
couldn't have protected her, that a poppy
tucked in her hair couldn't have saved her
from those German storm troopers?

This frightens me. I see eyes peeping
through narrow slats of cattle cars
hurrying toward forever. I see "Jude"
& "Star of David" scribbled across a depot,
but she says, That's the name of a soccer team,
baby. Red climbs the hills & descends,

hurrying out to the edge of a perfect view,
& then another, between white & violet.
It is a skirt or cape flung to the ground.
It is old denial worked into the soil.
It is a hungry new vanity that rises
& then runs up to our bleating train.

I am a black man, a poet, a bohemian,
& there isn't a road my mind doesn't travel.
I also have my cheap, one-way ticket

to Auschwitz & know of no street or footpath
death hasn't taken. The poppies rush ahead,
up to a cardinal singing on barbed wire.

Three Figures at the Base of a Crucifixion

— after Francis Bacon

Look how each pound of meat
manages to climb up & weigh itself
in the wobbly cage of the head.
Did the painter ascend a dogwood
or crawl into the hold of a slave ship
to get a good view of the thing
turning itself inside out beneath
a century of interrogation lamps?

It was always here, hiding behind
gauze, myth, doubt, blood, & spit.
After the exhibit on New Bond Street
they walked blocks around a garden
of April roses, tiger lilies, duckweed,
& trillium, shaking their heads.
The burning of mad silence left
powder rooms & tea parlors smoky.

Brushstrokes formed a blade to cut
the hues. A slipped disk
grew into a counterweight,
& the muse kept saying,
Learn to be kind to yourself.
A twisted globe of flesh
is held together by what
it pushes against.

Last of the Monkey Gods

They moon temple ghosts, swinging on heavy doors.
They ride rabid dogs in the alleys of ill repute.
They decipher the language of crows at dawn
in ancient trees, the blueness of a god's skin.
They tiptoe power lines, rope bridges around the city.
They throw stones at the ambassador's sedan.
When afternoon prayers begin, they grow silent,
lying in each other's arms, dreaming of clemency.

The monkeys are now rounding up street boys.
At least, at first, it seems this is true, but in no time
the boys learn to single out a monkey in the throng
& wrestle him to the ground. He may try to bite
& scratch, to howl & cry ceremoniously, to plead
with the one word he knows, but then the fight
goes out of him when the rest of his great clan
returns to jabbering & the sacred picking of lice.

The boys zap him with a small laser gun.
A garnet of mute bells is tossed into the dust,
& chants go aeons back to the beginning & die.
The fearless illumination goes out of his eyes.
The boys tag him. He rises to wander freely.
As naked unholiness crawls into the night,
they're wrestled one by one to the ground
& castrated for the music of coins jangling in a pocket.

A Visit to Inner Sanctum

A poet stands on the steps of the great cathedral,
wondering if he has been a coward in hard times.
He traveled east, north, south, & seven directions
of the west. When he first arrived on the other side
of the sea, before he fell into the flung-open arms
of a long romance, the lemon trees were in bloom.

After a year, poised on the rift of a purple haze,
he forgot all the questions he brought with him.
Couldn't he see the tear gas drifting over Ohio
as flower children danced to Jefferson Airplane?
Will he ever write a sonnet dedicated to the memory
of four girls dynamited in a Birmingham church?

Standing in the cathedral again, in the midst
of what first calibrated his tongue — gold icons
& hidden jaguars etched into the high beams —
he remembers an emanation almost forgotten.
He can't stop counting dead heroes who lived in his head,
sultry refrains that kept him alive in the country of clouds.

Underneath the granite floor where he stands
loom the stone buttresses of an ancient temple.
When he was a boy, with his head bowed
close to the scarred floor, he could hear voices
rising from below, their old lingua franca
binding with his. How could he forget?

Outside the Institute of National Memory
he toasts the gods hiding between stanzas.
The girl he left behind for enemy soldiers
to rough up & frighten, she never stopped
waiting for him, even after she lost herself
in booze. Now he faces a rusty iron gate.

Did she know someday he'd question a life
till he held only a bone at the dull green door
of an icehouse where they stole their first kiss?
To have laughed beside another sweetheart
in a distant land is to have betrayed the soil
of dispossession hidden under his fingernails.

Supposed he'd pursued other, smaller passions
singing of night dew? The dead ones kept him
almost honest, tangoing with wives of despots
entranced by stolen light in his eyes & hair.
He never wanted to believe a pinch of salt
for a pinch of sugar is how scales are balanced.

SEAN O'BRIEN

November

November is a book of subtle virtuosity. O'Brien's skilled handling of rhythm, structure, narrative and image are on full display in this latest collection, rich in evidence of a careful, elegant mind at work. In *November* we approach year's end, a time of reassessment, of clear-eyed stock-taking and redirection. "Look away just for a moment. / Then look back and see…" are the book's apt opening lines. This turning away and back, this existential strophe and antistrophe, are like the picked-through furrows of a ploughed field where O'Brien paces us with a firm hand past sites of sober reckoning. Gates, graveyards, stations, junctions and the hazy light of more than one afternoon bar become sites of conciliation with both past and present, where "every failure brings you its account / for signing." Placed in these terrains of transition, peopled by the dedicatees of elegy and homage, *November* affirms, through accumulated detail, these disappearing worlds that "cannot be other than real."

Sunk Island

She stares down the dead straight mile, at a walk,
While I stand by the lych-gate to let her
Arrive at this slow-motion replay of England.
Can I help you? asks the lady on the horse.
And I don't say: too late, unless your powers include
Self-abolition. *Me? I'm waiting.* I don't say:
Leave me be to read your graves, to stand and think,
To hear the water taking back the frozen fields.

It's not my place to tell you what I mean.
Perhaps I've come to use the weather up
And look too closely at your groves of oak and ash.
But we both know the fact I'm waiting here
Is cousin to a crime. We hold each other's gaze.
Who for? her bladed helmet asks. Her horse has turned
To steaming stone. I think I hear the sea far off,
Like evidence that each of us might call.

And why? — For the flood to accelerate over this ground,
For your helmet to circle and sink like a moral,
For a rag-and-bone man with his cargo of trash
To come rowing past slowly, his mind given over
To practical matters, the pearls of your eyes
Unforgiven and sold at Thieves' Market
For sixpence and never once thought of again.
You must be cold out here, she says. I think I must.

Josie

I remember the girl leaning down from the sunlight
To greet me. I could have been anyone. She could not:
She was Josie, remember, and smiling — she knew me already —
Auburn gate-girl to the garden-world,
To the lilacs and pears, the first summer
Seen perfectly once, then never again. And she left.
The garden — the garden, of course, has gone under the stone
And I cannot complain, a half-century gone
Like the cherry tree weeping its resin,
The dry grass, the slab of white marble
The butcher propped up in the back yard to sit on —
Things of the world that the world has no need of,
No more than of Josie or me or that morning.
Still a child as I see now, she leaned down
To smile as she reached out her brown hands to greet me
As though this were how these matters must be
And would be forever amen. She was saying goodbye.
And I cannot complain. What is under the stone
Must belong there, and no voice returns,
Not mine and not hers, though I'm speaking her name.

The Citizens

We change the river's name to make it ours.
We wall the city off and call it fate.
We husband our estate of ash,
For what we have we hold, and this
Is what is meant by history.
We have no love for one another, only uses
We can make of the defeated.
— And meanwhile you have disappeared
Like smoke across a frozen field.

What language? You had no language.
Stirring bone soup with a bone, we sip
From the cup of the skull. This is culture.
All we want to do is live forever,
To which end we make you bow down to our gods
In the midday square's Apollonian light
Before we ship you to the furnaces
And sow you in the fields like salt.

We fear that the fields of blue air at the world's end
Will be the only court we face.
We fear that when we reach the gate alone
There will be neither words nor deeds
To answer with. Therefore, we say, let us
Speak not of murder but of sacrifice,
And out of sacrifice make duty,
And out of duty love,
Whose name, in our language, means death.

White Enamel Jug

The Ardennes

There used to be a white enamel jug,
Its rim precise in Prussian blue —
Likewise the handle with its female curve
Through which a forage cap might fit: the jug
The maid's deserter drank from, slowly,
Boots off, his feet on the kitchen table,
Raising the thing like a trophy over his head
And licking his white cat-moustache,
While she kept waiting, trying not to laugh
At what a crime it was, behind him
In the doorway, naked, with her hand stretched out.
Midnight was all the time there was.
The stars froze, branches creaked, the cream
Sank in the jug, and so they took their happiness
For there and then and not for memory:
As, in his way, the Major also did
When he had sent his manservant to bed
And poured black coffee from this jug,
Then sat to write the letter home,
But paused, as though to read his palms
Within the circle of the lantern, while the jug
Attended, patiently, a kind of company
The night the war was lost, before
He rose and at the window watched the dark
Until at dawn the forest turned to flame.

The Lost Book

Here's where the far-gone Irish came to die
And having died got up to disappear
Into the space they wore into the air:
Smoke-room, bookies, God knows where —
They were a crowd who favoured solitude.
They came 'pro tem' and stayed, and stayed,
Bed-sitting room remittance-men
Whose files authority had usefully mislaid.
Dug out of 'kiln-baked' tombs, the gas left on,
This Tendency the calendar forgot
Kept suitcases of ancient paperwork
That could have grassed them up but didn't talk.
Poor demi-felons, dead of what? — of afternoons,
Whose rag and bone the council boxed and burned:
And you were of their party, were you not?

I owe you this. I watched you and I learned.
You lived provisionally, 'the man with no home team'.
Reliant on the Masonry of drink, you made
A modest and convincing entryist of crowds
Who only ever knew your Christian name,
Your trebles at Uttoxeter, perhaps
Your politics, on no account your game.
You seemed composed entirely of words.
'Tell no man — still less a woman — who you are.'
Who cares, now that the principals are dead
As the impossible morality
Whose prohibitions brought your lie to life
And in the end would send you off your head?
I care, for I was made to care.
You told a priest but couldn't tell your wife.
You were the author and the patient too,

And in another life another house
Imprisoned others and the clock had stopped.

You knew — and all you did was know —
That there was an appointment to be kept.
That was your art — to frame your punishment —
An endlessly extended sentence,
Solitary confinement in plain sight,
Nothing you could put down on the page,
Nothing you could ever simply name
But manifest in jealousy and rage
And episodes of heartbroken repentance.
There was nothing that could ever put it right.

'Yourself's a secret thing — take care of it,
But if it comes to handy grips you take no shit.'
Yours was a way of waiting, though you knew
That really there was nothing down for you
But vestibules and corridors and days
In which to seek permission to be old.
Kardomah Lampedusa, minus book,
Deported from successive realms of gold —
Longpavement and the Bronx and Hammersmith —
Or so you said, and who was I to ask?
Then when at last I came to take a look,
When you had sat it out as far as death,
Inside the case, behind the broken lock,
There were no secrets waiting underneath,
Just fragments of a poem you'd recite,
And scraps of stories you'd begun and re-begun,
In which the names alone would change, as though
You had forgotten who they were.

I found no history in this, no hidden world
Before I came — I'd heard your stuff bashed out
Through years of chainsmoked afternoons
And read it when you asked me to. I liked
The one where in the fog the sergeant found
His constable nailed up across a five bar gate,
But feared and did not understand the priest
In his deserted parish (fog again)
Who found his name had changed to Lucifer.
He lost his way and then he lost his mind
And that was that, with nowhere left to go,
Hell being where and who and what he was,
A state with neither origin nor end.

'The duty is to entertain,' you said, 'or else
To seek to make no sense at all.' And then
When you had filled the room with ash and smoke
There would be racing or the news, a second
Scouring of the *Telegraph*, a third, and no
Persuading you that you should persevere.
You were already old. Was that the plan?
To climb into the box and disappear
In smoke above the crematorium
And leave your furious pursuers unappeased
And shorn of purpose, standing in the snow
Beside the hearse, in mourning for themselves?

I studied you before the lid was sealed
And, as my mother had requested, placed
Rosemary for remembrance in your hands.
The deep, unhappy brow, the cloud-white hair
Combed back — oh, you were otherwise engaged.
In settling debts, or simply free to dream?
You wouldn't care to comment 'at this stage'.
Was there another world, where you belonged,

Or one more corridor where you still sit, rereading
With the patience of a lifetime
Last week's paper, hoping it might yield
To scrutiny and show the outcome changed?

Europeans

Now we are in Europe let us take
To selling mushrooms by the roadside,
Broad-brimmed platefuls and uniform buttons
Plucked before dawn in the forest of birch,
The dank delicious one-legged flesh
Climbing from grave-pits as big and as deep
As the forests themselves, for it does not
Take long to establish the custom, not long
To forget the beginning, to hold up
A bucket or basket of mushrooms
And talk about always and offer a shrug
That proves our knowledge and our ignorance
Identical, proverbial, entirely
Beyond the scope of history or law,
And since we have always been here
On our fold-away chairs near the crossroads,
Hunched in black overcoats, pale as our produce,
Seeking and selling the flesh of the earth
By the handful and kilo in brown paper bags,
We cannot be other than real.

Counting the Rain

Check the gas and hide the back door key.
Lock up. Make sure you have, and then
Go out and count the rain, and this time
Do it properly. You won't be home again.

Closed

No cigarettes tonight. No tea. The spoon
Swings on a chain from the counter's edge.
Every cup and saucer's full of ash.
The buffet is pretending to be closed.
Inside it, under glass, a sandwich waits for you.
Stay here too long and it may speak your name.
The revels are but lately ended, bab.
You thought you understood austerity —
But fuck your sympathy and go without.
The white-tiled Gents is like a ruined temple.
Now it takes the democratic piss,
And would you care for a discreet disease?
What day it is. What time it is. What sea-coast
And what realm is this. The roof
Upheld by iron trunks, the arches uttering
New arches, further demarcations of
The darkness in the ramifying dark. The chance
That this might be the secondary place, that home
Lies just across the footbridge, through an arch,
Along a platform looking up and down
The ordinary night — and *there*, a steamy door,
Change counted out in halfpennies, received
With patience and a joke that no one but
The waitress and her pink-necked soldier hear.
You had to be there, you suppose. You never were.
It's in the way you tell 'em, in the fact
You know so well what you could never find.

JOANNA TRZECIAK (translator)
TADEUSZ RÓŻEWICZ

Sobbing Superpower:
Selected Poems of Tadeusz Różewicz

Hearts can smart, and kindnesses be minded. *Sobbing Superpower*'s world-class document, compellingly assembled by Joanna Trzeciak, gives us an EKG-cum-EEG for an entire era — its double helix inscribed by that most sensitive device: a soul the equal of the world's occasion. A second global war had cast its blooming shade abroad, when Różewicz's carouseling lovers sang, on fabulous beast-back, in scarlet carnivale: "let us adjust the paper ribbons and wreaths / crouch down: let hip touch hip / your thighs are alive / let us flee let us flee." But Różewicz is himself too alive to history's evidence to pass off life and death as mutually exclusive. "Man is killed just like an animal / I've seen: / truckloads of chopped up people... // Concepts are only words: /... / truth and lie / beauty and ugliness / courage and cowardice. //... / I've seen: / a man...both / vicious and virtuous."

The etymological job of the skeptic: to keep an eye on things. Różewicz is that rare character — skeptic as full of passion as of intelligence, of warmth as wariness. Thanks to Trzeciak's deft, deferential translation, English readers see his place among stars of his Central-European generation — Herbert, Szymborska, Popa, Holub — poets who illustrate the power of a single plain-song to be heard over milling mobs; one sensibility to outweigh hours of broadcast nonsense; one oddball to resist the prefixed troopers; one poem's power to outlast the props of all sub-supers, super-subs.

Over sixty years, with grand themes but plain speech, with mortal passion but Heraclitic judgment, in torment and in tenderness, Różewicz proves as wary of philosophy's bureaucracy as government's; as wary of heaven's offices as man's.

Alert to our condition's own momentous momentariness, he's funny, fierce, or casual; but never inconsequential.

Unde malum?

Where does evil come from?
what do you mean "where"

from a human being
always a human being
and only a human being

a human being is a work-related
accident
of nature
an error

if humankind
disentangles
itself
from flora and fauna

the earth will regain
its beauty and lustre

nature its purity
and innocence

human beings are the only beings
who use words
which can serve as tools of crime

words that lie
wound infect

evil does not come from an absence
or out of nothingness

evil comes from a human being
and only a human being

we differ in thought — as Kant said —
and for that matter in being
from pure Nature

Homework Assignment on the Subject of Angels

Fallen
angels

look like
flakes of soot
abacuses
cabbage leaves
stuffed with black rice
hail
painted red
blue flames
with yellow tongues

fallen angels
look like
ants
moons wedged beneath
the green fingernails of the dead

angels in heaven
look like the inner thighs
of an underage girl

like stars
they shine in shameful places
they are pure like triangles and circles
with silence
inside them

fallen angels
are like the open windows of a morgue
like cows' eyes

like the skeletons of birds
like falling planes
like flies on the lungs of fallen soldiers
like streaks of autumn rain
connecting lips with birds taking flight

over a woman's palm
wander
a million angels

devoid of belly buttons
they type on sewing machines
long poems in the shape
of a white sail

their bodies can be grafted
onto the trunk of an olive tree

they sleep on ceilings
falling drop by drop

1964–1968

Love Toward the Ashes

What sprouts out of the ashes of
Samuel Beckett?

somewhere in this space is
his fading breath
and then a motionless utterance

in the beginning was the word
in the end the body

What decomposes? What suffers?
meat still full of love
spoils in time
stinks
one has to bury it

Ms. Peggy
(in a "memoir devoid of tact")
spoke of how he never got out of bed
before noon
"Oblomov" she called him
I am dead he would say
but Peggy says
they had
a great love affair

More Pricks Than Kicks
this title got him driven out
of Ireland
when I think of him
and I think of him often
I sense that out of his body

out of his jacket out of his pants
seagrass grows
just like out of an old mattress
lying in a dumpster
in a blind alley
but he did make a move after all
took his bed
flew to Berlin
and directed
three
of his own plays

iron discipline
every move calculated
in time and space
every creak of the floor
every breath on the stage
and in the audience
every hair on the head

he did not grant interviews
for hours he talked about soup
with his maid

sometimes I hear his fading breath
(his laughter never
reaches me)
as if the fur coat of Sucky Molly
were yawning shedding fur

and instead of
Virginia Woolf's
famed "birds of Paradise"
the room is filled with flies

Narcissus looked
in the mirror
and saw the head
of a predatory bird
of course he had parents of some sort
alas! even James Joyce
had mother father wife children
as happens in this vale of tears

Some time ago I read his poems
"*sans voix parmi les voix*"
"among the voices voiceless"
poems like any other
but who doesn't write poetry

too bad we will never
meet because I admired him
for the fact that he
breathed so calmly
awaiting the end of the world

but even he begins to bore

1982

Pig Roast

For Jerzy Nowosielski
a memento of our conversations about the killing of animals

"Remember that if the devil
wants to kick somebody, he won't do it
with his horse's hoof,
but with his human foot."

in a Swiss daily
I read an article
titled "Arme Schweine"
Poor pigs

how these innocent creatures
must suffer anticipating death
yet aren't our Polish pigs
as sensitive
as their Swiss sisters

En route to the slaughterhouse
they often die of heart attacks

in our country the pig roast is linked
with birth and death
with christenings funerals
and even first communion

In *Politics* I read an article
about transplanting a pig's heart
into a young man

"Of all things why did you settle
on a pig's heart?" asks the journalist.
"Based on size considerations,"
replies Professor Zbigniew Religa
from the Silesian School of Medicine;
"these were young individuals
weighing from 180 to 220 pounds
such that their hearts would be of human size…
and the Church condones
all transplants except for
brains
and reproductive organs…"

long live the pig!
friend of man
I sound this cheer
from the depths of my (human) heart

long live all pigs
eaten by humanity
since the dawn of creation!

how many pigs' hearts kidneys
how many pigs' feet
will be transplanted
by the end of the century

I ask as a moralist

can we find even one
man who would give his heart brain
or kidney to an ailing pig

when will humanity mature
into such love
that we could say
my sister sow

when will we build in Geneva or New York
in front of the headquarters of the United Nations
a monument
to a pig with her young

the competition for such a monument
I hereby declare open

Sobbing Superpower

(Saturday, January 20, 2001)

I'm reading Norwid

Over the mobile plains of the sea
I send you a song like a seagull, John

Long will she fly to the land of the free
Doubting she will find it so

I'm in Konstancin at a writer's retreat
talking with Ryszard Kapuściński
about Franek Gil
about globalization
we're drinking wine
I speak of population growth
he speaks of water shortages
not oil but water
not water
but lack of water will be the cause
of wars Ryszard says
blood will be spilled over water
not over homeland honor or god

it's gotten late

I hear that in far off
Washington it's sleeting
it's cold, foul weather
the new, 43rd president of the Superpower
is being sworn in
21-gun salute at the Capitol

The Superpower is sentimental
touchy-feely compassionate
("*mitfühlender Konservativismus*")
quick to tears

"compassionate conservative"
hand on Bible
the son of the 41st president

Abraham Lincoln looks on and listens

not even the downpour could
hide Bush's tears
the Superpower sobbed

The president's wife Laura wept
his twin daughters wept
the president's parents wept
former president George Bush
and his wife — Grandma Barbara
Gore's electorate wept
those who made sloppy holes
in the ballot cards
the holes that had to be counted over
the outgoing president
Bill Clinton wept his wife Hillary wept
(she wept but took the chairs
and loveseat wept but took the table
and curtains and who knows what else
…though she did give them back) their daughter
Chelsea wept Madeline
in a mini skirt a rose at her bosom
kept drying her eyes Bronek
wept too (but for different reasons)
the former

national security advisor
Sandy Berger
"kept reaching for his hankie"
the sky wept
vice president
Dick Cheney wept
as the 43rd president sheltered him from the rain
with his own coat
("compassionate conservative")
flipping up his collar
(to protect his own neck from the rain)

An obscure young intern wept
as did her mother who was left
with a soiled dress
in the closet
"My dear sweet child…"
what have you done?!
then there was a ball
made up of a hundred balls
and what a ball it was

for gentlemen the dress code was tails
and cowboy boots
or a tux
and cowboy boots

top hat or cowboy hat and cowboy boots

then there was a banquet
sixty-six hundred pounds of beef were consumed
(the old world would feel it in a few years
or even a few days)
fifty-five hundred pounds of ham
(also not a good omen)
and sixty thousand jumbo shrimp

the former president
bid the nation farewell yet again
again he apologized to the prosecutor and the nation
for lying about putting his finger where
it didn't belong
the finger for pushing the nuke button
don't catch your finger in the door!
promised to give back the chairs
and took off

the sky wept the earth wept
land and sea trembled
diplomats and generals
were blowing their noses

(the cardinals smiled shyly)

I too wept
reading the papers
then I listened to the radio
and laughed through the tears

Chiaroscuro

When shadow falls
on my poem
I see light in it
faint stubborn
a life

tiny death
takes its first steps
matures quickly
grows
at night lies
on my heart
on my lips
like a sea chiseled
in black stone

you were screaming at night
dreadfully
frightfully
my wife says

it was death drilling corridors
within me a living being
death screaming within me
like a deserted cave
full of bones

When light falls
on my poem
I see death in it
a black grain
of ergot

in a golden head of wheat
which drifts off
beyond the horizon

September 1983

CANADIAN
FINALISTS

KEN BABSTOCK

Methodist Hatchet

Babstock is the live wire in the gene pool: stirring things up, rocking boats, disjoining easier conjunctions, jolting the culture's DNA.

From sea-and-skyscapes literally lettered, from the suspect core of our "décors" ("lost heart" informs that fashion's stock and trade), he winds past mere mundanities to find the world again, with words for his divining wands. "Money's the more virtual virtual," Babstock writes. "I don't talk this way in real life."

Cable-stitched by shopping channels, across northernmost America and more, desire is wired: with HGTV's IV, or the PC's ICU, we feed our merchandizing minds. We bought this stuff, he says.

Disclosure's what he's after, as wary of the cosy center as of the so-called cutting-edge. But get a load of those poetic closures: master craft in "WikiLeaks and seasmoke" weaving worlds of words together. Man of letters, he remarks the X's on workmen's safety vests; the V's descending out of Gander, headed for the kind of down discounted in an Army-Navy store. A shapely mind will note the uppers, too; they're cut with aspirin and talc. This guy is one ferocious logophile.

A signature device, the "disconnected current gauge," trips all the switches: current cut off into currency—but also presents. It was "a gift," writes Babstock, with "its needle stilled between / 'Reverse clips' and 'Start charge.' Consult it / and it shivers on a hash mark."

Thus, in a flash, the disused item (mere décor) becomes occasion for a gift: the wordsmith talent, not the dollar sign, with other hashes hinted, other hushes marked. The old and new worlds hackable in just one comprehensive stun, this shock of shiver to be had. *Methodist Hatchet* lets us have it.

Thus do local gifts turn into global ones.

The Decor

Comes a time we all must aspire, no?
    Magazines declaring
in big sans serif: *Style, Interior, Form,* and
    Chair. Ok, I invented
Chair, but glossy spreads depicting
outrageously beautiful rooms

wherein one diminutive, three-legged, teak,
    mid-century stool
with a triangular seat and nubby
    cloth upholstery
of an unassuming meadow green
might very well cost

upwards of four grand. *Those* magazines.
    To the right of the chair
on the floor, a pile of stacked art books:
    Cindy Sherman, say,
Brice Marden, Gerhard Richter —
a Max Frisch novella

splayed on top like a stone bird on a plinth.
    I know, reading
the spines, I've entered into a kind of silent
    exchange
with the — what — art director? Nothing
now eases the buzzing

suspicion I'm being signalled to from across
    a great distance,
as in semaphore, or prayer. Someone
    wearing a Tag Heuer watch
swivelling behind a desk
in New York, or London,

wants very badly to trigger in me a visual
    of earned leisure in idealized
surroundings.
    Surroundings
that better describe how I'd already
long been picturing myself.

"It is not easy to write a familiar style"
    as Hazlitt had it. Then who
doesn't "hate to see a load
    of band-boxes go along
the street?" Corian slab in the calibrated
cubism of the kitchen,

brushed nickel, much is re-stressed, salvaged
    hangar door, its blast-
shadow of early corporate logo, laminate's
    blue-black is Reinhardt-deep,
a Chiclet gleam. Lucite "ghost chair"
blocking a view of chalk

petroglyphs. And isn't to picture oneself to mimic
    the distant highway
grader, slugging off toward rural anomie,
    appearing not smaller but
farther away, spitting at cattle, leaning
into work, overtaken and

honked at. Is this about style? I remember being
    warned ontology was ugly
by a poet who then ordered the chowder. Grass
    tells a story of listening
to Social Democrats and de-mobbed
Wehrmacht scrap it out

deep in a post-war mineshaft, headlamps
    casting flattened
versions of their huddle up against gouged
    rock wall, or ascending
cage panel, up toward sun-licked rubble, civic
life utterly fucked, but

somehow on the mend — That's a different
    magazine. My girlfriend
and I went halves on a chair and sofa set.
    Mid-century, yes, but knock-offs.
Nubby green upholstery, though
a green less meadow

than that mineral-rich, polyethylenized
    turquoise the Inside Passage
reflects seen from a ferry rail sailing south
    from Prince Rupert
to Port Hardy. You can see straight
through it to more of it.

The chair became our older dog's day bed.
    She'd roll into a brindled
donut, or flip and act the otter, her legs
    in air, head dangled as
counterweight over the armrest. A month ago
she chewed through

the fabric, a hole you could slide an arm into.
    Slide an arm right through
the surface of this picture,
        into whatever spatial realm lies
behind the illusion of depth, to hold
the hand of the person

wanting so badly to be seen precisely
        as they feel themselves
to be: launching, from over there, starched
        murmurs, mere vibrations
of air, in hopes they can correct the distorted,
over-adorned version

they fear you've displaced them with. And
        have you? Can you
know, lost in the forest of what J. L. Austin
        dubbed "medium-sized
dry goods": the bang, the furniture
the olufsson and clutter of

the manifest image? Sea-Dog, Redbird, bottled
        schooner, bug husks.
The disconnected current gauge was a gift,
        its needle stilled between
"Reverse clips" and "Start charge." Consult it
and it shivers on a hash mark.

Autumn News from the Donkey Sanctuary

Cargo has let down
her hair a little and stopped pushing
Pliny the Elder on

the volunteer labour.
During summer it was all *Pliny the Elder,*
Pliny the Elder, Pliny

the — she'd cease only
for Scotch thistle, stale Cheerios, or to reflect
flitty cabbage moths

back at themselves
from the wet river-stone of her good eye. Odin,
as you already know,

was birthed under
the yew tree back in May, and has made
friends with a crow

who perches between
his trumpet-lily ears like bad language he's not
meant to hear. His mother

Anu, the jennet with
soft hooves from Killaloe, is healthy and never
far from Loki or Odin.

The perimeter fence,
the ID chips like cysts with a function slipped
under the skin, the *trompe*

l'oeil plough and furrowed
field, the UNHCR feed bag and restricted visiting
hours. These things done

for stateless donkeys,
mules, and hinnies — done in love, in lieu of claims
to purpose or rights —

are done with your
generous help. In your names. Enjoy the photo.
Have a safe winter

outside the enclosure.

Which Helmet?

With the glove on, her pixellated breast every
demonstrably offensive line about young plums
and buds budding. With the glove and helmet on, "her"
is a proposition. With the helmet on she likes it when I
read to her from the book of desires I wrote
with the helmet on. Under the glove and helmet,
day indiscernible from night and want from love.
The other helmet cues God whispering in his quadrant.
There's no visor or need of one on the God helmet;
face a mask of contemptuous ecstasies, road
map of heaven on earth and the helmet on.
There's a crash helmet and infantry helmet
over in the corner that no longer fit as the head
of the poem has developed macrocephallicly.
Our universe, said to be coming apart at the seams,
poorly made, a *Jofa* from the mid-eighties, placing
us, like Butch Goring's head, at no small risk.
Jousting viable with the helmet on with the helmet
on time soups finally and selves sift. Horizons converge
in the mouth under the helmet and the glove
grips them like floss. This is Helmut Lang; I got
it at a consignment store. There's a Spartan
helmet behind glass; there's not much on it.
The helmet you were born
with very nearly obsolete, its list of incompatible
attachments growing longer by the day. Take trees,
for instance. Think of all the songs. Think of all the songs
without a helmet on and how they seem to weep
torrents over nothing for no reason. Put this on. Put
this on feel time die bewildered, binary, purchased
but no purchase gained, drainage
streaming out over the chinstrap.

Hoping Your Machine Can Handle the Big Image

Look, at an indeterminate juncture
  of my sixth year, I was moved to wed my purpose
to the graphic depiction of man

combing sense out from the knotted tangle of necessity

with event. 4H, or Jader Seed, or the Rotary
  Club had sponsored a poster campaign, on the theme
of farm safety, and I'd been inclined to think

of myself as *above the herd* when it came to one dozen

Crayola, arrangement of interpretive glyphs,
  primitivist use of prime colour, perspective, and
the slightly flattened, lowercase "m"s flocking

persistently up- and outward to a sheet's NNE

corner. I'd never, up to then, short of church-sponsored
  hay rides, been on a farm, or smelled the horneted,
chaffy old leather and striped light of a proper loft.

But how I ached to effect public opinion. I was earth

newly turned, baking in the heat of emergency;
  the very *un-safe*ness of harvest, the daily and flagrant
peril those agrarian classes toiled within shone into

my heart, drafting there an idea of justice in burnt sienna —

Initial concepts smouldered in the pitfire of the obvious:
  pitchforks were sharp, like needles, leaning
against barn walls, godless tridents, their eye-skewers

arced neglectfully outward. Flame and hay were like hay

and flame. Dung's greased, hazardous lubricant appeared
   underfoot pell-mell in pre-dawn's unpasteurized light.
It all either wouldn't boil down to pictorial shorthand,

or played like a back-forty Hanna-Barbera. I drew a hole.

A mare's ankle, twin toddlers, and five hogs disappeared
   like heat into the hole's black wax. I liked working
in gummy, spidered dust near the chewed and louvred

edges of wooden stair runners. Cereals, salted nuts, cinched

in a faux-naugahyde marble pouch. Crosscut, two inches
   thick, of hardwood, crenellations of bark stained red,
chapter and verse seared into its topographical map.

(Outside, Parmalat and Collier Grain turning the vise on small-
holdings by indirect means, Chicago tickertaped and bloating.)

Dreaming others' dreams of inheritance and succession

I filled the background with harvest wheat, pulled the blue
   wash down to meet its tips, then drafted a combine
in profile, forest green, mastodon mowing arabic land stalled

in cut stubble to spit from its spreader chute one

arm entire. Detached, serrated, pointing Cistinely at
        its drained farmer, stood lidless in the bib of shadow
his cap's beak cast. Stunned, regretful, disproportionate.

        Arterial leak of time in vermillion. Barn cats behind the silo

silo in front of the sun. Though I knew enough to make
        of his mouth a truncated line segment, the design
placed second behind a predictable gas leak and fireball.

Perspective means objects capitulate, finally, under
        prolonged grievance, to a visual rightness. I used
a straight-edge on each hexagonal lug-nut.

Avalon, Helicopter

Morning desacralized, the quack
science of fog. Moisture condensing
around airborne granules of salt, it's *cloud*
when we make out the silhouette

of a duck. Spit, the air
hits supersaturation and spits back. Gulls beyond
the first veil: clown's horn lashed
to the handlebars with stiff wire —

Hermit thrush on the near fencepost, beaded
meniscus in the bleached syringe.
Electroshock, duster, blot. One crow's drawn-out ablutions.
If Berkeley, as we hope, misfigured the contents, and ideas

are like other things, here, on a porcelain toadstool
sprouted from powerlines, is the sum of all past assertions
on essence. Underfoot sponge,
mystery mounds, moss ottomans, and everyone's addition

shearing away from first additions. Wild rose,
tin well cap, purple iris in the juniper tangle where a brook
bogs out from up on the cape's moonscape.
Shrew and owl. Confectioners

table of black shale where the clapboard claps out.
Tut's lost prick a wasp drips out of.
Whoever it was ransacked the ossuary built
this hitching post doohicky for the clothesline's antipodal pulley.

Scalded wrack. What's the local term?
Sippy cup in the shed
near the chainsaw and widowed oar.
Breaking the Bakelite surface out there,

a minke bends into the first, the only,
race gate — two grebes —
of his zen GS. On day one
of the home fishery, Michael, over a platter
of cod, "The real is not mental,
it's *mental*" as the pup tent fwaps, lifts anchor.

Evening's a tranche of kids on bog bikes,
Big 8 Cola, the dew line, Sikorski bolts,
Purity Crackers, WikiLeaks, and sea smoke.

PHIL HALL

Killdeer

Straddling the thin line between argument and lyric, the "Essay-Poems" of *Killdeer* are deceptively prosodic, and can switch from the stark and factual to short flights of startling, gorgeous lyricism: "Killdeer on my oozing stumps...Whipped the years' butcher block rings to crèche shavings...Her desperate ruse has settled into gunwales — her closed cry a prow's nib." Suspicious of artifice, surgically self-evaluating, Hall's poems at once pay tribute to writers and friends who have shaped his sense of integrity while analyzing his own progress and methods as an artist. A record of private and imaginative growth, *Killdeer* builds a powerful narrative of recognition, attesting to the introspective mind's capacity to transgress pain. This document of the examined life, through its hard-nosed accretion of realizations, is remarkably moving as it rows tenaciously between "islands of repair." Full of unease, gratitude, humour, intellectual and personal challenges, and not without bite, *Killdeer* is a testament to the creative life as an act of faith and transformation.

A Thin Plea

(Falteringly)

Our national bird — for years — was — as A M Klein said —
the rocking chair

I don't know what our national bird is now — but my totem bird is the killdeer

Its names — odd mannerisms — & cry — explain bits about me — in riddles

My daily writing self at 57 has accrued the usual odd habits & noises — there are awful names I know myself by — lie-dances I perform

In my hopelessness I half-hope my deflections might honour me

In open fields my bird ranges — it nests near cow plops & hooves — its only protection a desperate busking

If a person or a creature approaches its eggs — the killdeer pretends to have a broken wing — it flits near — then hovers away — one wing splints forward at an unnatural angle — its cry seems so plaintive

Intruders are diverted from its eggs by a chance at catching the adult

Like that wounded arrow-maker — Philoctetes — I have a broken wing — of sorts

Something wrong with my hands — eczema — nerves

My paints — red & dry — split along their lifelines — & bleed

It is difficult to wear white shirts — for instance

When I fall asleep I always go right back to the same fields I grew up in

Dreaming — I wander in those fields — my hands bleed into the furrows — I look for my eggs — I cry

I am not lying — but there has always been a hint of puppetry to my whining

I grew up on farms between Bobcaygeon & Fenelon Falls — mid-century — mid-Ontario — between Reaney's townships to the southwest — & Purdy's country slightly north to the east

When I write I am always mid-field — on one leg — the other poised over killdeer eggs

Have almost stepped on them again — but I hold the pose & write instead

Around me the bird cries its lies — as I hover there — pen poised

I am overcome & rejuvenated by imbalance — complexity

Its Latin name is *Charadrius vociferus* — a vociferous charade — its common name — *killdeer* — is a yoking of *precious* & *doomed*

*

Though you'd never know it to look here — I don't like to talk about writing — I always feel as if I am about to get slapped for showing off

My writing has been more about my life than my life has been about writing — the goal always better balance — a safer self — poetry has so little to do with writing

I'd rather talk about how you got your car started that cold morning — or about *your* writing — if you insist

I don't know where my eggs are — or what I am still so guarded about — or whether I even have any eggs still intact

I have hidden my poems in stumps — under floorboards — behind pseudonyms — in other people's books — in bus station lockers — under bridges — down my pants — & in my mouth

Like Yannis Ritsos I have put poems in jars & buried them on islands in Greece

I have put my poems in a Crown Royal bag — tied a length of binder twine to the bag's yellow cord — & then lowered the lot down a groundhog hole

Where the audacity to publish comes from — I don't want to know

Oddly — confession has figured in my writing — I have populated my poems with real people who would resent my use of them if they knew

I have operated on myself in public — I have abused language because I was abused

It's not true that I have saved my life by writing (though I often say so)

But I have — like the killdeer — made vaudeville of my pain — to distract my enemies — & this has distracted me too

I have hidden myself by pointing at myself — when the poems seem to point at actual scabs — they are pointing away

Coming from a bookless home — I have never gotten over an innate suspicion of text — even my own

I am being as honest as I can — though the hand itself is a puppet — a naked puppet

Give a pen to a naked puppet & ask it to write — in this case — the truth

In my case — you get an approximation of the killdeer — the pen is the beak

My pain — my pain — at first I thought that was what poets said

My pain — my pain — eventually I wanted not to mean it — now sometimes I don't mean it — but I say it anyway

*

Killdeer — there isn't much to say — just *here I am here I am*

Another waving of old tools as if they were broken wings

A thin plea *my pain my pain* — lies dying out in the dry grass — dying out in starlessness

A few small poems have stayed warm

*

My pain — my pain — I need a new bird — that will eat the old one

If I put cream on my hands each day — the holes close up

Years of not drinking — years of therapy — the gold thread of a third marriage — the inflatable anchorage of my children — these have healed me — not *cleverness* or *career* or *language*

What if all I know how to write is a cry — what if health has no poem — where are those goading — imaginary — enemies when I need them

*

Carl Jung said our great endeavour is to transfer the centre from ego to Self — capital S — this is what Killdeer has been up to — falsehood-altruism

My *IIIIIs* are too close together

I have come to trust choruses & group photos more than solos & head-shots

I would prepare my poems for a time when I won't be around to wave my cap to keep the flies off them

A poem — like a life — begins in ego — but it needs to move its centre to the Self

By this I do not mean that a poem should address universal themes — God no

I mean — cut the first person pronoun adrift — & the lyric will give up its addiction to pain

It may still be talking about pain — but it will have begun to circle — dithyrambic — in a field you are only one aspect of

Eventually the poem will ask you to give it away — like a bride — to its own imbalance & complexity

You will remember that *anon* has two meanings — nameless — & soon — getting out from under a name takes patience

*

When I can't sleep — when I'm sick — when no one else is home — when I'm lost in transit — I *tinker*

This is my word for what I do — a slow — un-clever — tactile — cheap — harmless rearranging of odd bits of wry nature & gatherings — until they sing — off-key

I tinker at long sequences — & stay close to notebooks — mostly when no one is looking

Am increasingly filled with hopelessness — but sometimes when I'm up to my elbows in a line's perplexities

Confidence lands its flocks upon me & I feel — inside the poem — unafraid

*

Killdeer on my oozing stumps has drummed her wings long & hard

Whipped the years' butcher block rings to crèche shavings —
beaten nests of feathered chips by simulated soar — folded herself
into my pages boatingly

Her desperate ruse has settled into gunwales — her closed cry a
prow's nib

The stumps' roots I thought destined to be fences — are a mob of
keels righting little brown-speckled eggs

Safe — adrift — hoving-to — as cloud-shadow swamps fields

The age of flight is followed by the age of sail

*

A new totem bird & I are just getting to know each other — it is
eating Killdeer slowly

Safer — healthier — silent — I sit in our rocking chair

Maybe I'll tell you what the new bird is called when I know

JAN ZWICKY

Forge

In *Forge*, Jan Zwicky performs a balancing act of great poise and beauty. An extended set of variations on the theme of listening, the collection pays repeated attention to music — and through it, to the natural world and human relationships. Love and death are topics almost too risky to address directly, especially with this kind of breathless, caught-up writing: the stakes could not be higher. Zwicky addresses them fearlessly, making them meaningful and felt, and borrowing the languages of mystery, even religion, to do so. The payoff is real and extraordinary. Gracefully sustained, her unashamedly lyric verse always feels earned by, and earthed in, lived experience: whether of grief or companionship, those great conditions, or, repeatedly, of a watery world. This is a book gauzy with images of condensation, meltwater, flood and mist. It also manages the rare trick of taking on music's abstract forms. For all her precision, this poet brings us close to the music of abstraction that lies near the heart of true verse.

Practising Bach

*for performance with Bach's E Major
Partita for Solo Violin*, BWV 1006

      PRELUDE

There is, said Pythagoras, a sound
the planet makes: a kind of music
just outside our hearing, the proportion
and the resonance of things — not
the clang of theory or the wuthering
of human speech, not even
the bright song of sex or hunger, but
the unrung ringing that
supports them all.

The wife, no warning, dead
when you come home. Ducats
in the fishheads that you salvage
from the rubbish heap. Is the cosmos
laughing at us? No. It's saying
improvise. Everywhere you look
there's beauty, and it's rimed
with death. If you find injustice
you'll find humans, and this means
that if you listen, you'll find love.
The substance of the world is light,
is water: here, clear
even when it's dying; even when the dying
seems unbearable, it runs.

LOURE

Why is Bach's music more like speech than any other? Because of its wisdom, I think. Which means its tempering of lyric passion by domesticity, its grounding of the flash of lyric insight in domestic earth, the turf of dailiness.

 Let us think of music as a geometry of the emotions. Bach's practice, then, resembles that of the Egyptians: earth's measure as a way of charting the bottomlands of the Nile, the floodwaters of the heart, as a way of charting life. Opera, Greek tragedy, Romantic poetry tell us that sex and death are what we have to focus on if we want to understand any of the rest. Bach's music, by contrast, speaks directly to, and of, life itself—the resonant ground of sex and death.

 And it does this not without ornamentation, but without fuss: the golden ratio in the whelk shell lying on the beach, the leaf whorl opening to sun, the presence of the divine in the chipped dish drying in the rack, *that* miracle: good days, bad days, a sick kid, a shaft of sunlight on the organ bench. *Talk to me, I'm listening.*

GAVOTTE

E major: June wind
in the buttercups, wild
and bright and tough.
Like luck — a truth
that's on the surface of a thing,
not because it's shallow, but because
it's open: overtoned.
Because it rings.
     Fate, too,
is character. But it's
the shape — the cadence
and the counterpoint. Luck
lives in the moment, and it
looks at you: the clear eye,
gold, when being sings.

MENUET I & II

*There's nothing special in it. All you have to do
is hit the right key at the right time.* Time:
that stream in which we do, and do not,
live. *Just practise diligently; it will all go well. You have
five fingers on each hand, each one as healthy as my own.*
Unison, the octave; the fifth, the fourth, the third.
Of the strings? The viola, if I have a choice.
At the keyboard, don't forget to use your thumb.
God's glory and the recreation of the mind.
*What I really need to know:
does the organ have good lungs?*
The partita of the world, the dance of being: *everything
has to be possible.*

BOURÉE

Partita, partie — a whole of many parts. Pythagoras, who is said to have studied with the Egyptians, is also said to have taught that enlightenment meant solving the problem of the One and the Many, of coming to grasp the divine unity of the world through its bits and pieces, as these come to us in language.

This may also be thought of as the problem of metaphor: that metaphor's truth, its charge of meaning, depends on the assertion of identity and difference, on erotic coherence and referential strife, on meaning as resonance and meaning revealed through analysis.

Lyric poets are always trying to approach the issue by forcing speech to aspire to the condition of music. Bach comes at it from the other end: he infuses music with a sense of the terrible concreteness, the particularity, of the world. And enlightenment? — Acceptance of, delight in, the mystery of incarnation.

GIGUE

    There is a sound
that is a whole of many parts,
a sorrowless transparency, like luck,
that opens in the centre of a thing.
An eye, a river, fishheads, death,
gold in your pocket, and a half-wit
son: the substance of the world
is light and blindness and the measure
of our wisdom is our love.
Our diligence: ten fingers and
a healthy set of lungs. Practise
ceaselessly: there is
one art: wind
in the open spaces
grieving, laughing
with us, saying
improvise.

When You Look Up

When you look up, or out,
or in, your seeing is
a substance: stuff: a density
of some kind, like a pitch
that's just outside the range
of hearing: numb
nudge of the real.
                        I saw air
once, in its nothingness
so clear it was a voice
almost, a kind of joy. I thought
of water — breath as drinking —
and the way it shows us
light. Or maybe it was light
I thought of — as though
water were the solid form
of wind, and air
a language with a single word
transparent to the world.
Your glance is this,
meltwater, mountain light.
The plunge and thunder of the pool.
The ripple at its farthest edge.

Schumann: Fantasie, Op. 17

Everything already lost: this always
is the moment where we must begin.
Ecstasy: the self's ghost
standing where you left it, paralyzed,
aghast, and joy, praise,
flooding your lips, your fingertips, the voice in you
huge and exquisite, its mouth
on the nape of your neck.

The west light, the north storm,
to have known, not to have known:
because that touch was silence
and the body is your home,

you will be named,
you will be seen,
the wing will open in you,
breaking. You,
caught in the slipstream of
your own bright anonymity,
you will be spoken to,
stunned, helpless, the wave rising through you
in the dark. Don't
pull the curtain: let the black pane
see you: you,
in the mouth of the night.

Not knowing, knowing:
each worse, each holding
decades in its hand: kitchens,
dumb jokes, kindness and the shine
on the knob of the gearshift in the February sun.
If there were a sword, a block, you think
you'd lay your head along that coolness,
close your eyes. But no,
the blood springs elsewhere, touch
flooding you with silence. You are born
and born again into your life.

*If I were able, love,
to be with you eternally*, if all things were
already lost. *Take then
these songs I sang you,*
north light, darkness, home, the ache
of the invisible and the pine trees
resinous with sunlight in the afternoon. O, the silence
in that naming, breaking
as you listened. And where the god stood inside you,
an empty shape, a wing.

Gemini

*after J. S. Bach, Cello Suite No. 5 in
C Minor*, BWV 1011, *Sarabande*

There is a life
in which I do not find you.

Handedness that does not know
it's paired, a voice
that does not recognize
its line as counterpoint.

As though I were to learn
the air through which I'd grown
had not been fluid, making room
for me, but that my life
had curled and trellised on
some absent shape of emptiness
that had the shape of you.

The stories of Stickwalking
God, or One-Side: half a man,
one leg, one arm. And yet
he is a marksman
and a hunter. Spear points. Tips.

His half a heart and
its unbroken love. They say
it leaps out from his side
each time it beats.

ABOUT THE POETS

KEN BABSTOCK is the author of *Airstream Land Yacht*, which was a finalist for the Griffin Poetry Prize and the Governor General's Literary Award, won the Trillium Book Award, and was a *Globe and Mail* Top 100 book; *Days into Flatspin*, which was shortlisted for the Winterset Award for Excellence in Newfoundland Writing; and *Mean*, which won the Atlantic Poetry Prize and the Milton Acorn People's Poetry Award. Ken Babstock lives in Toronto, Ontario.

PHIL HALL's first small book, *Eighteen Poems,* was published by Cyanamid, the Canadian mining company, in Mexico City, in 1973. Among his many titles are: *Old Enemy Juice* (1988), *The Unsaid* (1992), and *Hearthedral — A Folk-Hermetic* (1996). In the early 80s, Hall was a member of the Vancouver Industrial Writers' Union, and also a member of the Vancouver Men Against Rape Collective. He has taught writing at York University, Ryerson University, Seneca College, George Brown College, and elsewhere. He has been poet-in-residence at Sage Hill Writing Experience (Sask.), The Pierre Berton House (Dawson City, Yukon), and elsewhere. In 2007, BookThug published Hall's long poem *White Porcupine*. He is a member of the Writers' Union of Canada, and lives near Perth, Ontario. Recent books include *An Oak Hunch* and *The Little Seamstress*. In 2011, he won Canada's Governor General's Award for Poetry for his most recent collection, *Killdeer*, a work the jury called "a masterly modulation of the elegiac through poetic time."

DAVID HARSENT has published eight collections of poetry. *Legion* won the Forward Prize for Best Collection 2005 and was shortlisted for both the Whitbread Award and the T. S. Eliot Prize. His *Selected Poems* was published in June 2007 and was shortlisted for the Griffin International Poetry prize. *Night* appeared in January 2011. Harsent's English versions of poems written under siege in Sarajevo by the Bosnian poet Goran Simic have been widely praised. His collaborations with composers (most often with Harrison Birtwistle) have been performed at the Royal Opera House, the Aldeburgh Festival, the Royal Albert Hall (Proms), the Concertgebouw, The Megaron (Athens), the South Bank Centre and Carnegie Hall. Harsent is Visiting Professor at Hallam University, Sheffield, and a Fellow of the Royal Society of Literature.

YUSEF KOMUNYAKAA's thirteen books of poems include *Warhorses* (FSG, 2008), *Taboo* (FSG, 2004), and *Neon Vernacular: New and Selected Poems*, for which he received the Pulitzer Prize. He teaches at New York University.

SEAN O'BRIEN has written six collections of poetry, most recently *The Drowned Book* (2007), which won the Forward and T. S. Eliot prizes. *Cousin Coat: Selected Poems 1976–2001* appeared in 2002. His other work includes the book of essays *The Deregulated Muse* (1998), the verse plays *The Birds* (2002) and *Keepers of the Flame* (2003) and a verse translation of Dante's *Inferno* (2006). In 2008 his collection of short stories *The Silence Room* was published, followed in 2009 by his novel *Afterlife*. He is Professor of Creative Writing at Newcastle University.

TADEUSZ RÓŻEWICZ was born in Poland in 1921. He is a major poet and playwright.

JOANNA TRZECIAK's translations include *Miracle Fair: Selected Poems of Wisława Szymborska*, winner of the Heldt Translation Prize. She lives in Cleveland, Ohio.

JAN ZWICKY is a musician, philosopher and award-winning poet. In 1999, she won the Governor General's Literary Award for poetry for *Songs for Relinquishing the Earth*. Her most recent collection of poetry, *Thirty-Seven Small Songs & Thirteen Silences* (Gaspereau Press, 2005), was nominated for the Pat Lowther Award and the Dorothy Livesay Prize. Zwicky currently teaches philosophy at the University of Victoria.

ABOUT THE JUDGES

HEATHER MCHUGH was born in San Diego, California. She has published volumes of poetry, translation and essays, and for over 35 years has taught and lectured at universities. She is Pollock Professor of Poetry at the University of Washington, and one of the original visiting faculty at the fabled Warren Wilson MFA Program in Asheville, NC. In 2001, she and Nikolai Popov won the inaugural International Griffin Poetry Prize for their translation of *Glottal Stop: 101 Poems by Paul Celan*. In 2009 she was named a MacArthur Fellow. Her most recent volume of poetry, *Upgraded to Serious*, was published in the US and Canada.

DAVID O'MEARA was born in Pembroke, Ontario. He is the author of three collections of poetry, and a play, *Disaster*. His most recent book is *Noble Gas, Penny Black*. His work has appeared in a number of magazines and anthologies, including *The New Canon*, and *The Echoing Years*, a co-Irish/Canadian anthology. He has been shortlisted for the Gerald Lampert Award, the ReLit Prize, the Trillium Prize, a National Magazine Award, four Rideau Awards (theatre), and was twice winner of the Archibald Lampman Award. He is director of the renowned Plan 99 Reading Series, a founding director of VerseFest, Canada's International Poetry Festival, and will be poetry instructor at the Banff Centre in September 2012. He continues to tend bar at the Manx Pub in Ottawa.

FIONA SAMPSON is a poet, essayist and critic whose most recent books include a new edition of *Percy Bysshe Shelley* and *Music*

Lessons: The Newcastle Poetry Lectures. Published in more than thirty languages, she has eleven books in translation including *Patuvachki Dnevnik*, which was awarded the Zlaten Prsten. In 2009, she received a Cholmondeley Award and was elected an FRSL; she has since been elected to the Council of the Royal Society of Literature. She has received the Newdigate Prize, Writer's Awards from the Arts Councils of England and of Wales and from the Society of Authors, and has been shortlisted twice for both the T. S. Eliot Prize and Forward Prizes. She is currently Distinguished Writer at the University of Kingston and Visiting Research Fellow at the Institute of Advanced Studies, University of London. Her critical survey of contemporary British poetry, *Beyond the Lyric*, will appear in autumn 2012.

ACKNOWLEDGEMENTS

The publisher thanks the following for their kind permission to reprint the work contained in this volume:

"The Decor," "Autumn News from the Donkey Sanctuary," "Which Helmet?," "Hoping Your Machine Can Handle the Big Image," and "Avalon, Helicopter" from *Methodist Hatchet* by Ken Babstock are reprinted by permission of House of Anansi Press.

"A Thin Plea" from *Killdeer* by Phil Hall is reprinted by permission of BookThug.

"A View of the House from the Back of the Garden," "Blood Alley," "Scene One: A Beach," "Spatchcock," "Blue," and "Contre-jour" from *Night* by David Harsent are reprinted by permission of Faber and Faber.

"The Story of a Coat," "When Eyes Are On Me," "Poppies," "Three Figures at the Base of a Crucifixion," "Last of the Monkey Gods," and "A Visit to Inner Sanctum" from *The Chameleon Couch* by Yusef Komunyakaa are reprinted by permission of Farrar, Strauss, and Giroux.

"Sunk Island," "Josie," "The Citizens," "White Enamel Jug," "The Lost Book," "Europeans," "Counting the Rain," and "Closed" from *November* by Sean O'Brien are reprinted by permission of Picador.

"Unde malum?," "Homework Assignment on the Subject of Angels," "Love Toward the Ashes," "Pig Roast," "Sobbing Superpower," and "Chiaroscuro" from *Sobbing Superpower: Selected Poems of Tadeusz Różewicz* by Tadeusz Różewicz, translated by Joanna Trzeciak, are reprinted by permission of W. W. Norton.

"Practicing Bach," "When You Look Up," "Schumann: Fantasie, Op. 17," and "Gemini" from *Forge* by Jan Zwicky are reprinted by permission of Gaspereau Press.

THE 2012 GRIFFIN POETRY PRIZE ANTHOLOGY

The best books of poetry published in English internationally and in Canada are honoured each year with the $65,000 Griffin Poetry Prize, one of the world's most prestigious and valuable literary awards. Since 2001 this annual prize has acted as a tremendous spur to interest in and recognition of poetry, focusing worldwide attention on the formidable talent of poets writing in English. Each year the editor of *The Griffin Poetry Prize Anthology* gathers the work of the extraordinary poets shortlisted for the awards and introduces us to some of the finest poems in their collections.

This year, editor and prize juror David O'Meara's selections from the international shortlist include poems from David Harsent's *Night* (Faber), Yusef Komunyakaa's *The Chameleon Couch* (Farrar, Straus, and Giroux), Sean O'Brien's *November* (Picador), and Tadeusz Różewicz's *Sobbing Superpower: Selected Poems of Tadeusz Różewicz* (Norton), translated by Joanna Trzeciak. The selections from the Canadian shortlist include poems from Ken Babstock's *Methodist Hatchet* (House of Anansi Press), Phil Hall's *Killdeer* (BookThug), and Jan Zwicky's *Forge* (Gaspereau Press).

In choosing the 2012 shortlist, prize jurors Heather McHugh, David O'Meara, and Fiona Sampson considered almost 500 collections published in the previous year. The jury also wrote the citations that introduce the seven poets' nominated works.

Royalties generated from *The 2012 Griffin Poetry Prize Anthology* will be donated to UNESCO's World Poetry Day, which was created to support linguistic diversity through poetic expression and to offer endangered languages the opportunity to be heard in their communities.

The Griffin Trust

Margaret Atwood
Carolyn Forché
Scott Griffin
Robert Hass
Michael Ondaatje
Robin Robertson
David Young